Facing Discouragement

Kathleen Fischer
and
Thomas Hart

Paulist Press
New York/Mahwah, New Jersey

Cover/book design and interior illustrations by Nicholas T. Markell.

Library of Congress Cataloging-in-Publication Data

Fischer, Kathleen R., 1940–
    Facing discouragement / Kathleen Fischer and Thomas Hart.
        p.   cm. — (IlluminationBooks)
    Includes bibliographical references.
    ISBN 0-8091-3753-4 (alk. paper)
    1. Consolation. 2. Encouragement—Religious aspects—Christianity.
3. Depression, Mental—Religious aspects—Christianity. 4. Spiritual
life—Catholic Church. 5. Catholic Church—Doctrines. I. Hart,
Thomas N. II. Title. III. Series.
BX2350.2.F497   1997
242′.4–dc21
                                                            97-36844
                                                            CIP

Published by Paulist Press
997 Macarthur Boulevard
Mahwah, New Jersey 07430

Printed and bound in the
United States of America

Contents

IlluminationBooks

A Foreword

Whenthis series was launched in 1994, I wrote that Illumination-Books were conceived to "bring to light wonderful ideas, helpful information, and sound spirituality in concise, illustrative, readable, and eminently practical works on topics of current concern."

In keeping with this premise, among the first books were offerings by well-known authors Joyce Rupp *(Little Pieces of Light...Darkness and Personal Growth)* and Basil Pennington *(Lessons from the Monastery That Touch Your Life)*. In addition, there were titles by up-and-coming authors and experts in the fields of spirituality and psychology. These books covered a wide array of topics: joy, controlling stress and anxiety, personal growth, discernment, caring for others, the mystery of the Trinity, celebrating the woman you are, and facing your own desert experiences.

The continued goal of the series is to provide great ideas, helpful steps, and needed inspiration in small volumes. Each of the books offers a new opportunity for the reader to explore possibilities and embrace practicalities that can be employed in everyday life. Thus, among the new and noteworthy themes for readers to discover are these: how to be more receptive to the love in our lives, simple ways to structure a personal day of recollection, a creative approach to enjoy reading sacred scriptures, and spiritual and psychological methods of facing discouragement.

Like the IlluminationBooks before them, forthcoming volumes are meant to be a source of support—without requiring an inordinate amount of time or prior preparation. To this end, each small work stands on its own. The hope is that the information provided not only will be nourishing in itself but also will encourage further exploration in the area.

When we view the world through spiritual eyes, we appreciate that sound knowledge is really useful only when it can set the stage for *metanoia*, the conversion of our hearts. Each of the IlluminationBooks is designed to contribute in some small but significant way to this process. So, it is with a sense of hope and warm wishes that I offer this particular title and the rest of the series to you.

–*Robert J. Wicks*
General Editor, IlluminationBooks

Preface

*J*ob got a heavy dose of it. Teresa of Avila struggled with it for years. Even Jesus knew it at times. Discouragement seems to be an intrinsic part of the human condition. Though it comes in different shapes and sizes, it touches us all, regardless of age or status.

In preparing to write this book, we looked again at the discouragement we ourselves have known:

—in our work, hoping to have helped someone only to discover that we had failed to do so;

—in our marriage, tackling the same issues repeatedly after thinking we had them solved;

—in our families, facing one illness or crisis after

another, never quite getting the relief and breathing space we long for;

—in our prayer, ever falling short of the ideals we set for ourselves.

As we pondered these experiences, we asked ourselves: What exactly is discouragement? How does it come about? What resources help us deal with it? We invite you to walk with us as we explore these questions.

We begin with the meaning of the term itself, and then consider some of the individual and communal circumstances that leave us feeling discouraged. Along the way, we share ideas drawn from both the spiritual and therapeutic traditions for coming to terms with it. We found ourselves returning often to the love and compassion of God, the care we offer one another, and the love we give ourselves as the foundation of any success in moving through discouragement, no matter how it arises.

We hope you come away from these reflections more able to face the discouraging times in your own life, and better equipped to assist others who struggle.

Chapter One

What Is Discouragement?

God, all that I long for is known to you,
my sighing is no secret from you;
my heart is throbbing, my strength deserting me,
the light of my eyes itself has left me.
                    –Psalm 38:9–10

When we first discovered the music of Italian opera composer Giuseppe Verdi, we wondered where he could possibly have gotten all that he was pouring forth. How did his spirit find its way to such depth, power, and sublime beauty? As there is almost always an intimate link between the life experience of human beings and their works, we looked into Verdi's story.

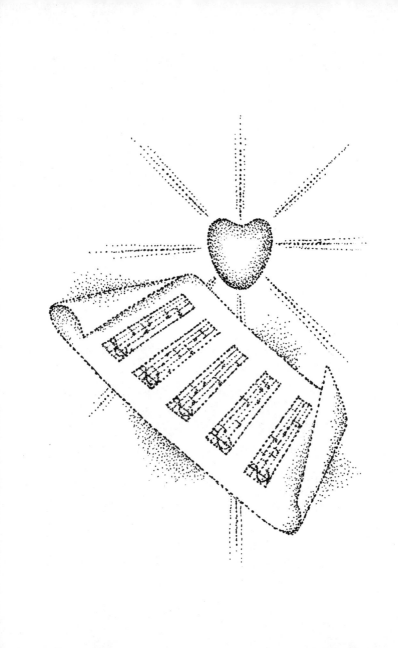

We learned that at the age of twenty-three Verdi married his childhood sweetheart, and within two years had a daughter and a son. During this period he also wrote his first opera, which was very warmly received. All was well. Then suddenly the wind changed. A childhood illness carried off his daughter. Then his son died. Shortly thereafter his wife was seized with encephalitis and she died. During the two year period that his entire family was wiped out, Verdi was under contract to produce a comic opera, which he somehow managed to do. But the opera was roundly booed at its premier (Verdi was present) and panned by the critics. He vowed he would never write again, and simply withdrew from life.

After this had gone on for a while, a friend who knew Verdi's prodigious gift tried to interest him in a libretto he had drafted for a new opera, begging him to compose the music. He had all he could do to persuade Verdi to take the text home and at least look it over. A very depressed composer reluctantly took it along. As he scanned the libretto that evening, he began to hear a melody in his head. The next day he wrote the music for one of the opera's choruses. Then more melodies came, and Verdi eventually set the entire libretto to music. This third work of his was a great success, and Verdi was back on track. He went on to give us some twenty-five operas. He also remarried.

This is a story of death and resurrection. There is a time of profound discouragement, during which Verdi visits the depths of hell. Eventually there comes a moment of conscious choice, and Verdi chooses life. But now we have a different Verdi. Because of all he has been through, he is a far deeper person than he was. And he goes on to fulfill his destiny, bestowing on us gifts of art that will renew the human spirit forever.

What Verdi suffered is certainly more acute than the discouragement most of us experience. Yet such times are familiar to us all. Our hearts grow heavy, and we feel like giving up. What is the use? Our way is dark, and all the sap seems to have drained out of us. We feel like failures; we just never get it right. No one can help. Hurt, rejected, robbed of what is most precious, we are beset with a sadness that will not go away. We are alone in a barren world. And just when we most need faith, we seem not to have any. God is remote, if God even exists. Death seems very appealing, if death were only a sleep.

Such experiences are common. Sometimes a relatively small event can cast us down, though of course it does not seem small at the time. What exactly is discouragement?

The root of the term tells us much. Inside the word *discouragement* lies the word *courage,* and inside the word *courage* sits *cor,* the Latin word for *heart.* Whether our discussion is about discouragement, encouragement, or courage, it is the *human heart* that is at stake. Discouragement is the loss of heart. Encouragement is the giving of heart. It is in the heart that hope and strength reside, the blood of life. Discouragement is literally "losing heart."

Discouragement is a miserable state. Yet it seems to be a normal part of life. Have you ever met anyone who has not known discouragement? Jesus himself, the man with the beautiful vision and the huge heart, got very discouraged at times. Surely he was discouraged when a crowd, rabid for a pitiless stoning, brought him a terrified woman caught in adultery. Jesus bent down and wrote silently on the ground (Jn 8:6). How did he feel when, after countless signs he had worked in their midst, the scribes and Pharisees came to him and asked for a sign (Mt 12:38)? The immense resistance he encountered in Jerusalem brought tears (Lk 19:41). Was ever a person more thoroughly crushed than Jesus, crucified for his pains, and apparently all alone in his death agony: "My God, my God, why have you forsaken me (Mt 27:46)?" Yet he is the very one who comes now to console us when we're down.

What does the bible say about discouragement? Are there other stories besides Jesus' from which we can learn? Yes, the bible knows discouragement well, and has much to say to us.

The bible and discouragement

A single line in Paul's Letter to the Romans sums it all up, offering us a perspective from which to read all of scripture:

> Indeed everything that was written long ago in the scriptures was meant to teach us something about hope, from the examples scripture gives of how people who did not give up were helped by God. (Rom 15:4)

Apparently Paul sees hope as the point of all the biblical stories. He is probably thinking about all the people who faced the problems of life and were tempted to give up.

Sarah had been promised a son, but her childbearing years were over now and there was still no child. The whole people had been promised a land of their own, but for years now were wandering through desert land with nothing in sight. Promised land? And when, after forty years of this, they finally arrived at habitable terrain, they found it already occupied by other people with armies arrayed against them. Generations later, when they strayed from God's ways as they were wont to do, Jeremiah was sent to speak to them, and he found no hearing whatsoever. Profoundly discouraged, he groaned:

> Woe is me, my mother, for you have borne me
> to be a man of strife and dissension for all the
>   land.
> I neither lend nor borrow,
> yet all of them curse me.
> Truthfully, Yahweh, have I not done my best to
>   serve you...? (Jer 15:10–11)
> You have duped me, Yahweh, and I let myself be
>   duped. (Jer 20:7)

These are not the words of a happy man.

More generations go by, and Mary and Joseph, parents of a child supposedly destined to save his people, are marooned right back in Egypt, driven there by a plot on the infant's life. Yes, discouragement was a very familiar experience to Israel's people, collectively and individually. Paul knew it well. He also knew that in every case, things eventually worked out—though not usually the way people expected. And one day it dawned on him that the whole collection of sacred stories had the same theme: hope. They were told again and again around campfires and in family dwellings and, because they all inspired hope, eventually set down in writing. Everybody realized how badly we need such stories because again and again our experience of the world disheartens us and we lose hope. Faith is no easy virtue. Battered by adversity, it loses its footing. We sorely need stories that remind us to tough out the hard times, stories that remind us God is faithful and always brings us through:

> A woman in childbirth suffers because her time has come; but when she has given birth she forgets the suffering for joy that a child has been born into the world. So it is with you: you are sad now, but I will see you again, and your hearts will be filled with joy. (Jn 16:21–22)

The anatomy of discouragement

When do we typically lose heart? Several common situations come to mind.

1. We have worked at something for a long time and have still not gotten the result we want. For example, we have put a lot of effort into a significant relationship and are still not seeing much improvement. Or we need a job. We have sent countless résumés, followed up with phone calls, and apparently it has all just disappeared into the wastebasket. Sometimes an interview raises our hopes, only to dash them again. Perhaps it is not a job but a life

partner we seek. We have gone through years of failed relationships and fallow periods between. Nothing has panned out. We might as well just give up.

2. We have worked hard at something and thought we were making progress, and then comes a setback. We studied hard for an exam, or labored long over a paper, satisfied we had done well. Back comes a low grade. We are crushed. Or we have done a lot of therapy and begun to feel we were getting free. Then something happens, and we find ourselves feeling and behaving just exactly the way we did when we began all this. Our heart sinks. Or we have poured all our energies into raising our children well, sacrificed and spent and patiently toiled. They seem to be doing well. Then suddenly they drop out of school, or get in trouble with the law, or tell us angrily how poorly we have parented them. We are devastated.

3. Sometimes several problems hit at once, and it is just too much for us. A friend was scraping along financially when his truck broke down. His truck was his livelihood, so he had no choice but to borrow the money and fix it. Then his dog, companion of many years, fell sick and died. Not long afterward he threw out his back at work and was sidelined for several weeks. Then his relationship with his girlfriend ended painfully. He was on the verge of despair, and who could blame him? What an extraordinary flood of misfortune. Perhaps we have not faced such a string as this, but we have all had the experience of many troubles coming at once and taking our strength away.

It would certainly seem that discouragement is the human spirit's worst enemy. For one thing, it is a miserable state to be in. And because it robs us of heart, it usually paralyzes action, putting a stop to a lot of good we might otherwise do. Discouragement is clearly a temptation, a state of mind to be resisted and overcome. We are no good for ourselves or anybody else when we are discouraged; we need to throw off the poisonous mood and get going again.

But before we push it away, it is always useful to ask if it might be carrying a blessing for us too. It may be telling us something we need to know, inviting us to some change we need to make. If, for instance, I am consistently discouraged as I go about my work, it might mean I should change my place of work, or even my line of work. What if I failed to listen to that? If I am constantly discouraged about my parenting, it may be that I am asking the impossible of myself, or of my kids, and need to revise my expectations. Or perhaps I need to change my approach. If I have long tried to make someone my friend, and they very rarely reach back, it may be time to stop beating my head against a wall and move on to other possibilities. Didn't Jesus counsel his disciples to give up and move on at times, as when some town would not listen to their preaching (Mt 10:14)?

But it is not just the message or invitation discouragement may contain that blesses us. Even when it carries no message beyond the fact that what we are doing is difficult, it blesses us the way any adversary does: by forcing us to dig deeper into our own resources and to open to the grace we are being offered. Jesus, for example, did not see the opposition he encountered as an invitation to turn aside from his mission and do something else. He embraced it as a challenge to his resourcefulness, his courage, and his hope.

Daily he took it to prayer and deepened his grounding in the One who strengthened him. Few great works are accomplished without much toil and in the face of formidable obstacles. Like Jesus, we grow through the things that we suffer. By grappling with discouragement and wrestling it to the ground, by taking it to prayer for God's direction and strength, we too grow in courage, hope, and grounding in God. It seems we have to go through many winters and springs to become truly beautiful.

Degrees of discouragement

Part of the anatomy of discouragement is the many degrees it exhibits. Human beings are creatures of moods. Circumstances can make us happy or sad, playful or angry, energetic or listless. So can the physiology of our bodies and the chemistry of our brains. This is true for men as well as for women. Some days we wake up sad or irritable with no apparent cause; sometimes there is an inexplicable wave of sorrow or desolation right in the midst of a generally pleasant day. There is not much we can do but weather these normal variations, continuing to meet our responsibilities and do what is good, whether we feel like it or not. These milder visitations make our lives more difficult, but they are not really crippling.

At the high end of the discouragement scale lies genuine depression, an abiding mental and emotional state that qualifies to be called an illness because it makes normal functioning nearly impossible. Sometimes it is precipitated by a heavy loss, such as the death of a loved one, the loss of one's job, sickness, or divorce. Sometimes depression is the product of the way we tend to interpret our experience, as, for example, when we take all the blame for anything that goes wrong in relationships, or when we overgeneralize from particular failures to the belief that we will never succeed at anything. Then it is our habitual patterns of thought that need to be challenged. But sometimes depression has a physiological root, a malfunctioning in the brain's chemistry that makes it extremely difficult to muster energy, think positively, interact socially, sleep normally, or concentrate on our tasks. When this is the case, we may need medication. And the good news is that, in recent years, a number of medications have been developed that assist our brains to function properly, making us feel much better and able to go about our business with far greater ease.

We are not talking about drugs that kill pain, help us forget, give us a high, or make walking zombies of us. We are describing medications that supply a deficiency, so that the habitually depressed person is simply put on the same basis most people are on most of the time. People who have been biochemically depressed for a long time are quite surprised at the difference proper medication can make; they never realized how bad they had felt most of the time. Suddenly, the door to a much more satisfying life swings open.

This kind of depression is often hereditary. So if you see depression in your extended family tree (and alcoholism is sometimes a manifestation of it), you are a more likely candidate. If you notice that you are usually depressed and do not know why, or that your depressions are recurrent, descending for no apparent reason and then lifting on some equally mysterious cue, you might well be suffering from depression that is physiological. An evaluation by a professional could help you ascertain this and get you the medication you may need. It might make a huge difference in your life.

Prayer

God of my life, help me to understand discouragement.

Help me to recognize that it is a normal part of life, that everyone has to battle it, that it need not defeat me.

Help me to remember that it always carries a blessing for me, that I grow through my struggle with it, that it may also carry a message for me.

Help me to recognize when I am bringing it on myself— by laying unreasonable expectations on myself and others, by comparing myself with others instead of accepting my own unique endowment and destiny, by looking too much on the negative and overlooking all the good.

You know how easily I can lose heart and give up.

Jesus, you knew discouragement too, and are with me always to strengthen me.

Help me triumph over my dark times as courageously as you did over yours.

–Kathleen Fischer and Thomas Hart

Chapter Two

Am I Enough Yet?

My own heart let me more have
pity on; let
Me live to my sad self hereafter
kind,
Charitable; not live this tormented mind
With this tormented mind tormenting yet.
—Gerard Manley Hopkins

An ancient Sufi tale tells of a stream that was working its way across the country, experiencing little difficulty.
It ran around the rocks and through the mountains. Then it
arrived at the desert. Just as it had crossed every other bar-
rier, the stream tried to cross this one, but it found that as
fast as it ran into the sand, its waters disappeared. After

many attempts it became very discouraged. It appeared that there was no way it could continue the journey.

Then a voice came in the wind. "If you stay the way you are you cannot cross the sands; you cannot become more than a quagmire. To go further you will have to lose yourself."

"But if I lose myself," the stream cried, "I will never know what I'm supposed to be."

"Oh, on the contrary," said the voice, "If you lose yourself you will become more than you ever dreamed you could be."

So the stream surrendered to the sun. And the clouds into which it was transformed were carried by the raging wind for many miles. Once it crossed the desert, the stream poured down from the skies, fresh and clean, and full of the energy that comes from storms.

*   *   *

Sometimes the most difficult periods of our lives are also the times of deepest transformation. But in their midst, hope seems a thin thread holding our lives together. Like the stream in this Sufi tale, we find our personal efforts blocked and can see no way to continue. Perhaps this discouragement is a signal to us that we need to let go if a new way is to open. What must die if we are to weather the storm of discouragement? We might begin by letting go of two things: perfection as the goal of health and holiness, and success as the measure of our worth.

Letting go of the ideal of perfection

Discouragement often results from setting our sights on being perfect. We determine to exercise more, pray regularly, curb our anger, become a better person. Like a string of ambitious New Year's resolutions, our good intentions soon give way to self-reproach. We lose hope. Our confidence plummets. The mirage of perfection holds out promise that one day we will be able to eliminate all the mistakes, imperfections, and failures that plague us. We will stand before God and others with everything perfectly in place, every crease and wrinkle smooth. Everyone will love us. So we chip away at ourselves, like a sculptor trying to get just the right form to emerge from the marble. But perfection is unattainable. We are imperfect people in an imperfect world.

As long as we cling to the ideal of perfection, we will never be enough in our own eyes. Inside each of us is a critical voice that is able to shred our best efforts. No matter how well we do, we could have done more. This inner critic draws our attention to each limitation, each flaw. Its voice is shrill and demanding, a composite of all the outer judges we have known in our lives: "You never do anything right. Look what a mess you made of things." "You ought to know better. How could you make such a stupid remark?"

Perfectionism thrives on comparisons. Yet nothing gets us down faster than measuring our achievements against those of others. In the process we almost always idealize others while minimizing our own gifts: "Look at how clean she keeps her house. And her kids are all doing so well. I'm so inadequate. What's the matter with me that

I can't hold it all together?" All in all, we find that we are never as good, smart, or efficient as others. Working harder does not help, as some defect always remains.

What would happen if we stopped striving for perfection? What if we were willing to embrace our reality whole? Perfectionism means we chisel out the weak place, get rid of the blemishes. Wholeness calls us to embrace all that we are, not only our kindness and diligence, but also our impatience and hardness of heart. This is the way of compassion for ourselves, and it was the way of Jesus. He looked with love upon imperfect and complex people: the Samaritan woman from Sychar, who, by the time she met Jesus, had had five husbands; his apostle Peter, who, when the stakes were high, could not find the courage to admit that he was a follower of Jesus.

Recently a young woman, her face drawn and tired as though worn out by stress and struggling, described how down she had felt all weekend. She had gone to the zoo with a friend. As they walked around, she noticed mothers and daughters having fun together. She felt jealous and angry when she thought of how her own mother had neglected her. This was not a new feeling, and she was mostly angry at herself that it had come back again. Hadn't she dealt with all of that? Why did she have to feel it again? She was upset with herself for going back to it.

Underlying our discouragement there is often a concept of personal and spiritual growth as simple and straightforward. We envision change as a direct line of progress, like an arrow that shoots straight for its mark. Life is, in fact, more like a rainbow than an arrow. It is a

PRECONTEMPLATION
CONTEMPLATION
PREPARATION
ACTION
MAINTENANCE

mix of sunshine and showers, a mix of the refraction and reflection of the sun's rays in drops of rain. Joy and sorrow lie close together in us, and to access one we often have to feel the other. We struggle most of our lives with the same weak and wounded places. A friend says she now knows the same failures are going to recur, and she is able to say, "Here it is again," rather than beat herself up for not having become a completely different person.

Does this mean that we should never try to change any of our behaviors? No, but it does caution us to be realistic and patient with ourselves in the process. When we are discouraged about finding ourselves backsliding, it is helpful to remember the limits of our usual models of personal growth. Growth is more like a spiral than a straight line; we circle back again and again to the same issues and struggles. And there are setbacks. In fact, a growing body of research indicates that we usually only succeed in breaking unproductive habits after three or four unsuccessful attempts. The path to change is a series of small steps. At every step it is simple things that keep us going: breaking a task down into very small parts, learning to laugh at ourselves, getting a good night's sleep, reading an inspiring book, creating a change of pace.

In working with persons trying to break addictions to nicotine, alcohol, and drugs, several stages of change have been identified. The first is *precontemplation*, when we have not given much consideration to making a change and may not even think we need to. Next comes the *contemplation* stage, when we begin to accept the idea that we might be better off if we made a change—for example, exercising more or setting aside a time for prayer each day. We next move to *preparation*, the stage at which we are convinced we need to change our ways, and have even taken a few steps in that direction. We then move to *action*, where we begin to make some changes, see their results, and look for support from relatives, friends, and colleagues. Finally, there is the *maintenance stage*, where we struggle with the tendency toward backsliding. At this stage it is especially important to realize that failures are not disasters. We rarely slide all the way back to our starting point, and each failure can teach us something about reaching our goal.

In her journal entry for October 12, 1942, Etty Hillesum talks about letting ourselves experience all of our inner seasons. As the forces of Nazi oppression moved into her native Holland, Etty, a Dutch Jew, began to keep a journal, later published as *An Interrupted Life*. She writes not only of the momentous events of her time, but of the daily challenges of life.

> And then again there are moments when life is dauntingly difficult. Then I am agitated and restless and tired all at once. Powerfully creative moments this afternoon, though. And now utter exhaustion.
>
> All I can do is to lie motionless under my blankets and be patient until I shed my dejection and the feeling that I'm cracking up. When I felt like that in the past, I used to do silly things: go out drinking with friends, contemplate suicide, or read right through the night dozens of books at random.

One must also accept that one has "uncreative" moments. The more honestly one can accept that, the quicker these moments will pass. One must have the courage to call a halt, to feel empty and discouraged. Good night.[1]

Like Etty, we repeat the same behaviors and contend with the same limitations all our lives. Yet they are never really the same. We are different each time we return to these issues. Native American spirituality offers us insight here. Its circular concept of time and space holds that all points in the sphere of being have a significant identity and function. We do not reach a fixed point and remain there; the universe moves and breathes continuously. Setbacks are intrinsic to the growth process. What matters is what we do with them. If we affirm ourselves for what we have done, and learn from what goes wrong, we can move on again. Acceptance of self remains an essential part of the process of change.

Love as the measure

Perhaps nothing is as powerful an antidote to discouragement as learning to love ourselves. Deep inside each of us is a longing to be loved, and a fear that we are not worth it. If we become beautiful enough, do the job well enough, we reason, we will please our parents, our teachers, our bosses, our friends. Then they will love us. This creates impossible expectations of ourselves. The roots of discouragement lie in our belief that we have to become lovable before we can be loved. In his comments on *Beauty and the*

Beast, G.K. Chesterton turns this conviction upside down. The truth is rather, he says, that a thing must be loved before it is lovable.[2] The experience of being loved is what helps it become more beautiful.

We can begin by giving this kind of generous love to ourselves. A first way to do this is to settle for being good enough—not perfect, not ideal, but a good enough parent, student, friend, human being. Often when we try to be just good enough, we end up being better than ever. Another way to love ourselves is to let our critical voices die by paying less and less attention to them, attending instead to that fragile inner voice that affirms and supports us. Inside each of us there is a gentle, kind voice that is like the crocuses of spring pushing themselves through the snow. If we give it space and nurturance, it will gradually grow stronger and fill the space now occupied by the critic. How does this voice sound? "Nice job," it says. "You did your best—that's all you have to ask of yourself," it tells us. Surely this is closer to the voice of God within us, the divine voice of which the Psalmist says:

> Whenever I remember your compassion, my heart is filled with joy.
> I know you see my affliction and understand all that troubles me.
> You will not abandon me to that which would harm me.
> You will set me in a safe and spacious place. (Ps 31:7–8)[3]

Our own compassionate voice opens to a power beyond itself, a gift of love, wholeness, and peace that we cannot fully give ourselves.

This divine power is our deepest resource in facing discouragement. Scripture shows this to be true for many people who find themselves in difficult times. There is the woman in Mark's gospel (5:25–34) who has spent all of her money on useless physicians, trying to get relief from internal bleeding. Twelve years later, her condition and suffering are no better; in fact, they are worse. She reaches out to Jesus and finds a power that is transmitted through love. It is her deep faith that opens her to the healing touch of Jesus. There is the witness of Paul, who knows from his own experience the truth of what he writes to the Corinthians, that "God's foolishness is wiser than human wisdom, and God's weakness is stronger than human strength" (1 Cor 1:25).

These biblical figures embody the paradox in the Sufi tale of the stream that must lose itself in order to become more than it has ever been. It is the paradox at the heart of the gospel: the losers end up as the winners. "My grace is sufficient for you: for power is at full strength in weakness" (2 Cor 12:9).

In his novel, *The Diary of a Country Priest*, Georges Bernanos also captures this paradox. He recounts the story of a devout and withdrawn young priest assigned to his first parish. Set in a little French village, the book tells of this idealistic priest's simple and difficult courage in the ordinary, small events of ministry. The backdrop to his courage is the despair and lethargy of the human situation, felt from the novel's first pages in the desolate November sky, the drizzle and thin, steady rain that dampens the village. The story is about the miracle of empty hands, the wonder that we give what we do not have. It witnesses to God's power within human weakness. This is captured in the young priest's final words as he is dying. Upon learning that a priest will probably not arrive in time to give him the last rites of the church, he says: "Does it matter? Grace is everywhere...."[4]

Prayer

When a voice within me
finds little to praise,
belittles my projects,
and shreds all my gifts of body and mind,
Word of Life, speak to this chaos within me,
   touch me with your tenderness.

When love seems a prize
awarded the few,
for which I must strive
straining toward the best
but coming up short,
Compassionate Friend, hold me in your love,
   comfort me with your grace.

When I grow weary at heart,
wonder why I should try,
become restless and anxious,
fearful of failures,
and fall back where I started,
Healer God, free me from my fears,
   and send me on my way again.

          –Kathleen Fischer and Thomas Hart

Chapter Three

Necessary Losses

Now can one learn to live through the ebb-tides of one's existence? How can one learn to take the trough of the wave? It is easier to understand here on the beach, where the breathlessly still ebb-tides reveal another life below the level which mortals usually reach.

—Anne Morrow Lindbergh,
Gift from the Sea

Life is always moving, and there is little we can hang on to. Life is good-bye, life is hello, as the title of a book on grief puts it. Do not cling, the wisdom of the East has long counseled. But this is no easy teaching. "If you try to save your life, you will lose it," Jesus says, enjoining the same idea. But living with such loose hands and so forward-looking a spirit takes a certain faith in God's providence.

In this chapter we will look at some of the passages practically everyone goes through in the course of life. These are not the familiar passages—leaving home, establishing a new family, midlife, career change, aging, dying—so well treated in many places. We speak rather of significant transitions that take place inside of us, could come at almost any age, might in fact occur more than once in a lifetime. They affect, respectively, our relationship to God, to self, and to the world.

The funny thing about passages is that there are no clear road signs that declare, "Here begins a transition in your life." We are some distance into a passage before we realize that something has happened. But there is a reliable internal indicator of change: discouragement. Because our accustomed approach to life is no longer working and we cannot make it work, we lose heart. Discouragement here serves its benevolent function: warning light, wake-up call. It causes us to take stock of our situation.

Losing our faith

Sometimes we feel we are losing our faith. We can no longer accept some aspect of church teaching or practice that had never been a problem before. Or the God who used to guide and comfort us is now too long away. Or a calamity befalls us or a person we love, and our belief in God's goodness and concern seems impossible to sustain. Deprived suddenly of a crucial support, we feel very discouraged.

These are actually very normal disillusionments, part of the maturation process. Our experience broadens, our awareness deepens, our reflection is not satisfied with the simpler answers of former times. We are not losing our faith but expanding it. And it needs to stretch if it is going to be able to embrace all of our growing knowledge and experience. We once asked a physicist after the Easter Vigil how he heard the readings about the seven days of creation and the parting of the Red Sea. He said that when he listened to such readings he turned off everything he knew scientifically and just believed the readings as they stood. Most of us cannot do that, and it does not seem like a good approach anyway. We need somehow to reconcile all the different areas of our knowledge into a unified vision of reality. And this means that the faith of our childhood needs to keep pace with the rest of our advancing experience. It needs to become adult.

Raised as children in the Christian faith, of course we believed that God sent ten successive plagues upon the Egyptian people (because they were not chosen), and spoke with Moses face-to-face the very words that Moses later wrote down. We believed we had our own guardian angel always at our right side, with the devil on the left side. We may also have been taught that if we did anything impure, and that included any looks, touches, desires, or thoughts, it was a mortal sin, and if we died before we could get to confession we would spend all eternity in hellfire.

If we cannot believe any of this anymore, at least not in the way we originally conceived it, have we lost our faith? At times it has seemed so, and that is the alarming and painful experience we are talking about. It is no fun to see any of these cherished childhood notions run up against the doubts occasioned by a more mature experience. When they do, we either revise our notions or lose respect for the whole package as the stuff of childhood. But if we jettison the whole thing, we have lost that which gives meaning and direction to our lives, and are left poor indeed.

Our life of prayer is another area where we can easily experience discouragement. In the early stages of the spiritual life, prayer is often easy and pleasant, filled with God's consolations. Then the going gets tougher, with far fewer times of comfort or enlightenment. We wonder whether prayer is still worth setting time aside for, as nothing seems to happen during it, nobody but ourselves seems even to be there. Our mind wanders. Even when it is present, there is nothing there for it to focus on but blankness. We lose heart. We start to blame ourselves. Maybe we just do not know how to do this. Maybe God is rejecting us. And little wonder. Why should God bother with so ordinary, so unspiritual a person?

Here is where some spiritual reading can help us. What we learn from those who have gone before us, including the greatest of the mystics, is that this apparent barrenness is part of everyone's spiritual journey. Sometimes it goes on for years, even in the lives of the saints, and is, generally speaking, more the rule than the exception. God is silence. God is mystery. God cannot be manipulated. And God's way of dealing with us, in our prayer as in our whole life, is beyond our understanding. "Be still and know that I am God (Ps 46:10)." We have to learn to let God be God, and this does not come easily. We have to be content with our best effort. It is still worth going to prayer, no matter how poor it seems, because we do make contact with God there whether we feel it or not, and it does have a good influence on the rest of our life.

Each of these successive bumps in the spiritual life, whether it be in our prayer, our way of believing, or our image of God, is a transition from what is smaller to what is larger. Each is a death and a resurrection. For God is always greater than our thoughts. We need our images, stories, and concepts; they convey crucial truths to us. But they are never adequate to the mystery they besiege. They are the formulations of human mind and imagination, striving to capture what cannot be captured. God keeps teaching us this as we live along, and the ongoing disillusionment, though it feels like the loss of God, is really a benevolently guided journey deeper into the truth.

Losing false selves

There is another passage in life, a wonderful one, to a much better place. Yet it too is born of pain and discouragement, and makes arduous demands. It happens when we discover that we have been living off our true center, and need to find our way back home.

Many a woman falls in love, and her whole concern becomes pleasing a partner. At first it is wonderful. The pain of it creeps up slowly, may take years of marriage to make itself felt. But one morning she wakes up and asks herself: "Why is he the earth, and I the mere moon? This isn't fair." And she is right. That day is her birthday.

Now she begins the journey back to her own

forgotten center. She begins to ask herself, "What do I feel? What do I think? What do I want? Who am I?" She feels selfish as she asks these things. It is all so new, so contrary to her conditioning as a girl and the life she has been living for many years: "Take care of everyone. Please them and they will like you. Don't make waves." But it is not selfish. She has just as much a right to life as anyone else. It is God-given. And her destiny, like everyone else's, lies in living out of her own true center, and doing her loving from there. This news is good, almost too good to be true.

At the same time it is difficult. It is not so easy to discover what she really thinks, what she really wants. Few have ever asked her, and she is very underpracticed. What is worse, when she finds it and summons the courage to say it, some people don't like it. Her husband, for instance. It is all new to him, too, and very challenging. It is not as convenient as their old life used to be, and he will have to grow some before he can understand and endorse what is happening in her.

Meanwhile, this whole experience of disapproval, of being labeled uppity or angry, is very hard on her. Accustomed to getting strokes from pleasing everyone and being thought very nice, it crystallizes for her that she is forced to a hard choice: "I can continue to please them all, at cost of myself; or I can live the life that is authentically mine, at cost of their approval. I cannot have both." She will have to grow, gradually uncovering more of her self, enduring feelings of false guilt ("selfishness") until her earlier conditioning gradually fades, learning to live with incomprehension or disapproval as natural accompaniments of authenticity.

But the journey is worth it. "What does it profit you if you gain the whole world but lose your *self* (Mk 8:36)?" In the original Greek of the New Testament, soul and self are one and the same word.

We write of a woman's journey here because this is such a typical struggle for women. But all of us, and more than once, have this experience of discovering that we are off our personal center. We are living inauthentically and need to find, nurture, and express that true self within that is God's original creation. Feelings of discouragement are the tip-off to the problem.

Losing our illusions

Sometimes it is our illusions of happiness that are the source of our discouragement. A very common one is the illusion that if we could just get it right, our problems would drop away and life would be smooth, as it is for other people.

As it is, our problems are multiple and persistent. There is not enough money. Our work is boring. Relationships are difficult. The car is giving out. We are lonely. We must be doing something wrong. If we could just get it right.

The best line in a generally good book, *The Road Less Traveled*, is the very first: "Life is difficult." End of paragraph. This is a fundamental truth, the author insists. There is no getting to easy street because there is no such place. Even wealth and beauty will not get us there. Neither will a degree, the mate of our dreams, or retirement from the drudgery of work. Life is difficult, has been since birth, will be till death. Accepting that truth is the beginning of wisdom, the essential foundation of such happiness as we may enjoy in this world. The real enemy of our peace is the illusion of some elusive magic formula. That our lives are filled with problems, that challenges just keep coming, is neither our fault nor does it make our lives different from other peoples', for we are all the same in this regard. Only the details vary. This may be a discouraging fact, but not as discouraging as the persistent search for an escape from the human condition when there is none.

Another illusion is the persistent idea that I must have some particular object of desire for my happiness. Marriage is a common one. Single people pine for marriage, living as if they do not have a life because they are not yet married. What they forget is that all kinds of married people would like nothing better than to be free of their marriages.

It can go the other way too—a happy marriage and then a terrible loss. A woman whose husband had died many years before came for counseling. She brought photos of him, letters. She wanted to talk only of him, of his struggles in life, of her failures to love him well. She had come, she said, to gain new insights into him. It soon became evident that she was living in the past and wanted to stay there. She was trying to keep him alive by building a shrine to him and pouring all her energies into him. This is tragic. Their love was undoubtedly true, her loss great, the loneliness keen. We do need to grieve our losses, and when a long and happy marriage ends in death, the grief is terrible. But this woman was making a life of it. Her husband had been dead for years.

Tom's sister describes in a poem this struggle we all have with letting go.

When I was very young,
No more than seven springs,
I used to capture butterflies,
And hold their trembling wings
within my tiny hand.
And then I'd let them fly again.
I did not understand the why of it,
but sensed, in growing,
I had no right to halt their going.

Now, being older,
closer to winter than to spring,
I found a butterfly in you,
And for a moment, just as then,
I did not want to let you go.
You charmed me so.
But I am wise as any child
And know I have no right
to stop or slow your flight.
The strings I used to bind all things
are even looser now,
so when I say, You're free,
I know you'll go.
But even so,
I will have other springs,
and always the sweet remembrance
of having touched your velvet wings.[5]

Life is never in the past. The past is gone. Life is in the present, and in the future God is always creating for us. Do not cling. In Anthony de Mello's words, life is like a symphony: it has great moments, but you never stop it, otherwise you cannot hear the whole work.

The enlightened person knows that we need next to nothing for our happiness, because our happiness is within us. We do not have to be the best at what we do. We do not need to have our own home. We do not need our youth. We do not need any particular person. We do not even need our health—though this is probably the greatest challenge of all. Happiness does not depend on any of these things. We find it within ourselves. It springs up naturally when we come to the present and enjoy what is here, now. It breathes freely inside of us when we stop making ourselves miserable by focusing on what we do not have and thinking we must have it.

It is perfectly all right to have preferences. Health, friends, and the things money can buy are genuine goods; they do give us pleasure. It is when we make a preference into an *indispensable condition* that we lose our lives. And we have lost them to a common illusion.

There was a wonderful cartoon in The *New Yorker*. Two people sit on a deserted island in the sea. They sight a raft approaching with two people on it. "A raft! We're saved!" they exclaim. Meanwhile, on the raft, the other two people are exclaiming, "An island! We're saved!"

Prayer

Teach me, O God, the art of the open hand,
     receiving all things with gratitude,
     and letting them go again without fear.

Give me a trusting heart,
     open to the future you are creating for me,
     ready to work in concert with you to make it good.

Free me from my illusions,
     the madness my culture encourages,
     the subtler deceptions my own nature is prone to.

Let me not cling,
     to how I have believed,
     to what I have enjoyed,
     even to those I have loved.

I place my life in your kind hands.
     Help me to trust the process even when I do not
     understand.
     Help me to enjoy the entire symphony.

I return again to my own true center,
     where you dwell in the stillness,
     from which my direction comes.
          –Kathleen Fischer and Thomas Hart

Chapter Four

Surviving Life's Heaviest Blows

God is our shelter, our strength,
ever ready to help in time of trouble,
so we shall not be afraid when the
earth gives way,
when mountains tumble into the depths of the
sea....

—Psalm 46:1–2

We once had a student, a woman in her fifties, who used to pass out pieces of candy at odd times. She'd smile: "Have a little candy—to soften the blow of life." Everyone chuckled, but everyone knew exactly what she meant. Life is punctuated with various blows, big and small. Even the small ones seem big at the time they land.

But some stand up as large no matter how you look at them. They really throw us, and mark the beginning of a genuinely dark time. We refer here to any serious loss—job termination, the end of a relationship, serious illness or injury, the death of a loved one. How can we ever get over the loss of something that has been terribly important to us? And how do we sustain ourselves in a long, dark season? A second type of heavy blow is one that may have happened long ago, yet is still affecting our lives profoundly—serious abuse or neglect in childhood. A third is an outer condition that weighs heavy on the heart and from which there seems to be no escape—social oppression.

Crushing losses

Some losses are so terrible they leave us reeling. A huge hole has opened up, and we cannot imagine how our lives can be pieced together again in any meaningful way. We may not even care to go on living. The loss of a job might affect us this way. But the loss of our physical integrity through an accident, or the loss of health with the onset of a debilitating illness, cuts even deeper, because often there is no possible repair. There is certainly no replacement for a dearly loved person who is suddenly gone forever.

When such blows as these fall on us, we are pitched into grief. Much helpful material has been written on the grieving process, which we cannot reprise here. We want to emphasize three points that relate to the discouragement intrinsic to grief. First, hard as it is to believe, a person does get through it. We are surrounded by those who have, who are doing well now, who rebuilt their lives and have gone on. We can do it too, and God is there to help us. There lies an immense resiliency in the human spirit, as the poet Gerard Manley Hopkins reminds us so beautifully:

> There lives the dearest freshness deep down
> things;
> And though the last lights off the black West
> went
> Oh, morning, at the brown brink eastward
> springs—
> Because the Holy Ghost over the bent
> World broods with warm breast and with ah!
> bright wings.[6]

The second point is that there is no way out but through. Though we may get discouraged at our pace, we have to endure the suffering, move slowly through the stages. The feelings that swirl and roost are nearly all dreadful: sadness, anger, loneliness, envy, guilt, despair. There is little point in resisting them; each has its own validity, and they need to course through and abide awhile before they exit. We can push them aside, and must at times, in order to function as our responsibilities require. But we have to give them scope rather than repress them if we wish eventually to heal.

Thirdly, we need someone to share them with. They are too much to bear alone. It sometimes brings relief to express them in writing. But they cry out to be shared—with a friend, mentor, or therapist. And they will naturally be at the core of our prayer if we bring God what most concerns us.

At the end of the chapter, we will speak of ways to care for ourselves in these and other difficult seasons. But first, a couple of living parables.

A man we know, who lost his legs in the Vietnam war and navigates the world in a wheelchair, says it is his faith, along with the meaning he finds in his work, that sustains him. Always he is seeking the deepening of his spiritual life. He believes God has some purpose in everything, and that life is worth living even with the suffering it inevitably entails. He stresses the importance of inner choice, whatever sort of hand life may deal us to play.

> I can choose to be sad or angry. I can sink into self-pity, and play on the pity of others. I've discovered I can easily use my handicap as an excuse for not doing what I don't feel like doing. I've done it. But I don't have to be that way. I can fight off the discouragement, and maximize the positive. I feel much better when I do. I know that God wants me to enjoy life and use my gifts. That is basically my faith, and that is what keeps me going.

Sometimes on our walks we meet a blind woman who lives in the neighborhood. She hears us coming and greets us. She stops and introduces her dog. Then she realizes that we have already met. We exchange a few words. As we part, she smiles and wishes us a good day. What a beautiful spirit. She who could so easily be discouraged is paradoxically an encouragement to others.

Our ungrieved childhood

A major cause of discouragement, even of clinical depression, is an ungrieved childhood. All of us have incurred some damage in handling, but some of us, by abuse or neglect, were wounded deeply, and our wounds still need to be drained so they can heal. Therapy is the ordinary way to do this.

It may seem obvious that what was done or not done to us as children was not our fault. But to the child this was not obvious at all. If we were physically, sexually, or verbally abused, or seriously neglected, we almost certainly concluded within the very limited understanding we had that it was somehow our fault: it happened because there was something wrong with *us*. We were somehow *BAD*. This conviction that we are flawed at the core continues to haunt our adult self-consciousness, along with all the other effects that abuse or neglect had on us.

Now we need to do what the child would have done instinctively if he or she had had an available parent at the time: go to an understanding adult (usually a therapist), and cry out the pain. We need now what the child needed then: empathy, validation, encouragement. We need to be told again and again that the abuse or neglect was not our fault, and consequently that the self-hatred and feeling of badness is entirely misdirected. We need support as we feel and express all this stored pain, and as we go through the same emotional cycles any grieving person goes through:

anger, sadness, anxiety, guilt, and the disheartening fear that the anguish will never end.

That we may carry this kind of pain is not always obvious even to us, because already in childhood we learned to wall it off. But the wound has ways of making itself known. Sometimes we have unexplained physical symptoms: headaches, digestive problems, chronic pain. Sometimes there is inner anxiety or turmoil with no apparent cause, sometimes even panic attacks. Sometimes there is smoldering anger that lashes out at small provocations, or a merciless self-hatred that shows itself in self-destructive tendencies. Recourse to drugs or alcohol often just adds to our problems, but is perfectly understandable on the basis of our longing to deaden our misery.

Only when we have drained out the inner pain we have carried so long can we be helped to see that we have also been blessed by what we have suffered. God always works with us to bring all possible good out of evil.

> We rejoice in our sufferings, knowing that suffering produces endurance, and endurance produces character, and character produces hope, and hope does not disappoint us, because God's love has been poured into our hearts through the Holy Spirit that has been given to us. (Rm 5:3–5)

Often a deep and lasting relationship with God grows out of childhood loneliness. Also, the resourcefulness we developed because circumstances forced us to it is now an invaluable possession. A natural empathy for others who are suffering is another common legacy; in fact, many a helping career takes its rise from personal pain worked through. Our healing process is finished only when it has reached some measure of celebration.

The burden of oppression

Oppression is a great gray blanket lying over the land. Those complicit in imposing it may be unaware it even exists. But the oppressed feel its weight always—unless they have so bought into the ruling class's definition of reality that they do not recognize the wrong. Oppression afflicts whole classes of people. Black people are oppressed by white. Gay and lesbian people are oppressed by the straight majority. Women are oppressed by men. If you are a member of any of these classes, you know the pain of being thought less of, of not being respected or listened to on the same level as persons of the oppressing class, of being denied equal opportunity in crucial areas of life, of being in danger even of physical attack and abuse. These experiences, and they just keep coming, cast us down and drain the heart of energy. And there seems no remedy, because the state of affairs just goes on, wrongs are done every day, and those with the power to change things so often do not care.

What do we do when we cannot change the system and it is killing us? First, we *can* change the system, and we must. Who else will? We may not be able to do a great deal, but we can do something. And doing something is an excellent use of the energy our anger gives us, which otherwise so easily becomes a corrosive acid eating away our innards. Most of the great social changes accomplished in history have begun with very small actions taken by people with no great power. The nationwide movement that brought the war in Vietnam to an end started with the paltriest of demonstrations.

In the meantime though, while social change is slowly and imperceptibly taking place, we have to find a way for our spirit to rise above the oppression under which we live. We have to disown the definition laid on us by others, keep shaking off its contagion. We need the support of others. It helps to read those who name the injustice clearly, reject it, and remind us of our dignity. And we need living contact with other people in our situation who recognize what is going on and refuse to accept it. We also need to go before God every day, to experience again the unconditional love with which we are embraced as we are, and the dignity that is conferred on us by our Maker as our birthright. Externally, those who oppress us might at the moment have considerable power over us. But internally, they have only as much power as we give them.

Caring for ourselves

How do we get through a difficult season? When we know we are into a dark time, and it is going to last awhile, what can we do to help ourselves make it through? The following suggestions might point a way.

1. *Lighten the load where you can.* Think of how you would treat yourself if you were sick. You simply cannot do what you do routinely when you are well. What responsibilities can you shed for a while? Enlist the aid of a sympathetic

LIGHTEN THE LOAD

BUILD COMFORTS INTO LIFE

TAKE A BREAK

VISIT THE SOURCES OF LIFE

DIG INTO GOD

PRACTICE THANKSGIVING

friend to help you distinguish between what you absolutely must do and things you may feel committed to that for the time being really could be handled by someone else.

2. *Build some small comforts into your life.* There is pain aplenty, and if you are not careful you will get bogged down in it entirely. Plan small pleasures for your evenings and weekends—a bubble bath, comfort food, good music, a walk in a beautiful place, good reading, time with someone you enjoy. During such a season as this, you need some things you can look forward to. These may not be the specific items for you. What gives *you* pleasure? What renews *your* spirit? You need it now more than ever.

3. *Take a break.* Would you like to go away for a while? Is there any way you can arrange it? To the mountains, a lake, the ocean? To a retreat house? To visit a relative or good friend? This may or may not be possible. But you could at least take a day off once in a while. Or even a nap. Or ask to be left alone awhile so you can journal or meditate, if that is what refreshes your spirit. This is not the time for heroic fidelity to duty.

4. *Visit the sources of life regularly.* Those sources differ somewhat for each person, but there are some common ones. *Nature* renews us, especially those of us too much in an urban environment. Go where there are trees, where there is water. Go to fresh scents and scenes of color. Watch nature for its parables; it is filled with them. It was the principal source of Jesus' best ideas. *Children* are another wonderful life-spring. Go where there are children, if only to watch them. If there are children you can interact with, all the better. *The arts* are another life source—painting, sculp-

ture, literature, music, dance, architecture, photography, drama, movies. Which do you enjoy? The arts always reopen our eyes, remind us of the grandeur of existence. Artists are keenly aware of the tragic dimension of life and of human pain; but they plumb the deeper meanings, often touching the transcendent. *People who love you* are another source of life. People who accept you as you are, who do not judge, who rarely give advice, who genuinely value and enjoy you, with whom it has always been fun to share life. Spend time with them. Ask them to bear with you. You can bleed to them a little. But you need just as much to hear them talk of their world, of what they are up to and interested in. You need to stay connected to the bigger picture, where life goes on and people are finding it worth living. You will get back there yourself after a bit.

5. *Dig into God.* You need God. You are made for God. And there is probably no better time to cultivate a relationship with God than in a dark season.

> Come to me, all you who labor and are heavy laden, and I will give you rest. Take my yoke upon you, and learn from me; for I am gentle and lowly in heart, and you will find rest for your souls. For my yoke is easy, and my burden is light. (Mt 11:28–30)

> If any of you thirst, come to me and drink. If you believe in me, as the scripture has said, "Out of his heart shall flow rivers of living water." (Jn 7:37–38)

There is this Presence, deep inside you, with which it is a comfort to spend time. Go down there. It wants to hold you. Practice meditation, and you will not be so lonely. Read a book on it if you need to, or ask a knowledgeable person for some leads on how to do it. Do not worry about the fact that you have too much neglected God. You will find welcome. The Psalms are another way to pray. You can easily find a dozen of them that express exactly what your heart wants to say. They will also speak back to you God's comforting words.

6. *Practice the prayer of thanksgiving.* This form of prayer is much advocated in the New Testament, whose writers know well that everybody carries burdens and some are very heavy laden at any given time. How can you give thanks when you are feeling miserable? It is a stretch, but it ends up strengthening you. By pushing yourself to name all that you have to be thankful for, you experience again all the good things you have that you are forgetting. You realize that God does love and care for you. Now you can see your troubles in broader perspective.

Prayer

Sometimes I wonder, God, if I have ever accepted the conditions of life—that trouble is part of it, that I grow through my struggle with it, and that you are with me always to help me.

Help me to believe that it is all meaningful even when I cannot see the meaning.

Help me to remember that things do eventually work out, though not in the way I might wish or expect, that all the things I worried about so much in the past have somehow been resolved, and that this is the point not only of my story but of so many of the stories preserved for us in scripture.

I am shortsighted and easily shaken. I so often lose awareness of all the good things I have, and of all that is going well in my life. I forget how even the blows I have suffered through the years have somehow blessed me.

I do believe that one day I will be free of trouble at last, that glorious day when you will dry the tears from every eye.

It is all in your providence, O God. I will let you be God, and give the world's management back to you. Just give me a trusting heart.

–Kathleen Fischer and Thomas Hart

Chapter Five

Despair and Hope for Planet Earth

*S*pring seems far off, impossible, but it is
coming. Already there is dusk instead
of darkness at five in the afternoon;
already hope is stirring at the edges of the day.
—Kathleen Norris,
Dakota: A Spiritual Geography

Last night we watched the last lunar eclipse of this
century. As the earth's shadow slowly blanketed the
moon, the late September night's brightness became
increasingly dim. Finally the moon was fully obscured. We
were sure the big globe of lunar light was still there, its out-
line discernible behind earth's shifting veil. But we talked
of how this phenomenon must have felt to our earliest

ancestors who witnessed it for the first time, without any assurance that the shadow would pass and the moon's brightness be restored.

We witness a kind of eclipse on our planet today, one that we watch without knowing whether the shadow will, in fact, lift again. Many of us struggle not simply with discouragement but with near despair at the prospect of planetary extinction. Acid rain is killing our trees. Pollution is destroying our waters. Species are becoming extinct. And the human beings perpetrating this violence on nature are having just as much trouble getting along with one another. Random shootings occur on our streets and freeways. Wars and genocide continue without abatement. Nuclear disaster threatens all life. How can we not be heartsick in the face of such massive problems?

Discouragement often takes hold when we realize how large the problems are, and how seemingly feeble our efforts to solve them. Sometimes, gripped by a sense of futility, we simply pull tight the shutters and get on with our personal lives. We stop reading the paper, disregard the news, and try to ignore the rest of the world. While this might be a temporary reprieve, it is not a lasting solution. Nor is it the Christian vision.

Seeds of hope

During his time as pastoral leader of Seattle, our Archbishop Raymond Hunthausen used to share a favorite story that sustained his commitment to the peace movement during difficult times:

"Tell me the weight of a snowflake," a coal mouse asked a wild dove.

"Nothing more than nothing," was the answer.

"In that case I must tell you a marvelous story," the coal mouse said. "I sat on a branch of a fir, close to its trunk, when it began to snow—not heavily, not in a giant blizzard, no, just like in a dream, without any violence. Since I didn't have anything better to do, I counted the snowflakes settling on the twigs and needles of my branch. Their number was exactly 3,741,952. When the next snowflake dropped onto the branch—nothing more than nothing, as you say—the branch broke off."

Having said that, the coal mouse flew away. The dove, since Noah's time an authority on the matter, thought about the story for a while and finally said to herself: "Perhaps there is only one person's voice lacking for peace to come about in the world."

Most of those who work to alleviate suffering know times of deep discouragement. They also believe in the significance of small deeds. The mustard seed of the gospel lodges in their hearts and sustains their efforts, that seed "which at the time of its sowing in the soil is the smallest of all the seeds on earth; yet once it is sown it grows into the biggest shrub of them all and puts out big branches so that the birds of the air can shelter in its shade" (Mk 4:30–32).

When Dorothy Day, foundress of the Catholic Worker Movement, died in 1980, historian David O'Brien called her the most significant, interesting, and influential person in the history of American Catholicism. Countless thousands have been fed and sheltered in her Houses of Hospitality. Yet Dorothy saw her life as a series of small gestures, and her favorite saint was no grand reformer but the saint of "the little way," Thérèse of Lisieux. For St. Thérèse, the path to holiness consisted of performing, in the presence of God and for love, all the ordinary little actions that make up our everyday lives. From Thérèse, Dorothy learned that even the smallest act of love contributes to the balance of goodness in the world.

Another revered spiritual leader, Mohandas Gandhi, took the concept of nonviolent action and applied it on a massive social scale to achieve the independence of India. Any experience of India's teeming cities brings home what an achievement this was. And Gandhi's influence has spread far beyond India's borders, challenging women and men everywhere to love and respect the person of their enemies. Yet Gandhi insisted that he was a very ordinary person with less than average ability, and that each of us can cultivate such faith and hope. He reminded those of us who want to follow his path that almost everything we do will be insignificant, but it is very important that we do it. We are called to live nonviolently and to contribute to the world's welfare even if the improvement we seek seems unlikely or even impossible.

When the landscape is darkened by massive suffering and evil, we need faith in the power of small beginnings.

In *Dwellings: A Spiritual History of the Living World*, the Chickasaw poet and novelist Linda Hogan provides us a fragile image of hope against great odds. In Japan, she recalls, there were wildflowers that grew in the distant, cool region of the mountains. The bricks of Hiroshima, down below, were formed of clay from these mountains, and so the walls of houses and shops held dormant trumpet flower seeds. When the atomic bomb was dropped, flattening the city, a small miracle began to happen. Out of the crumbled, burned buildings, out of the destruction, the bomb heat, and the fallen walls, the seeds of the trumpet flowers broke open and began to grow.[7]

Acting together, held by God

Discouragement lifts when we join with others who care about the future. In her book, *Despair and Personal Power in the Nuclear Age*, Joanna Macy argues that we can find release from psychic numbness and despair in the realization that all life is interconnected. She believes it is our sense of isolation that fosters resistance even to hearing more information about the present planetary crisis. We do not even want to know about it because, left to our own resources, we have no idea what to do. It is therefore not enough to get more data or hear more overwhelming facts and figures.

In the sacred web into which we are all woven, we find others who are ready to work together with us, to risk with us in joint ventures. What one person cannot do alone, we can do with others—clean up rivers, plant trees, begin programs that support troubled youth. In this way

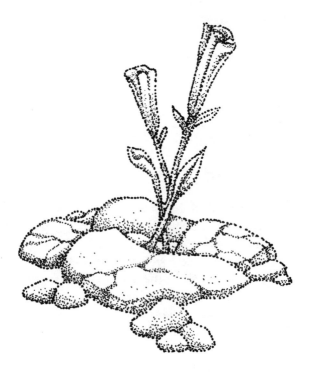

we find not only small solutions but we open ourselves to grace, the presence that is working through us. In this Presence the world and all of us who care about it are held and loved.

We often need reminders that God is with us in the struggle. So did our ancestors. We see this in the prophets of the exile: Jeremiah, Ezekiel, and Second Isaiah. In a foreign land, far from their homes and familiar surroundings, the people poured out their lament:

> Beside the streams of Babylon
> we sat and wept
> at the memory of Zion,
> leaving our harps
> hanging on the poplars there. (Ps 137:1–2)

In the midst of what seemed to be Israel's very dismantling, faced with the loss of temple, land, and faith itself, the prophets proclaimed a new beginning, with fresh actions from God. In response to the exhaustion and despair of their people, the prophets brought the divine promise. Where can we turn when all seems lost? What can we hang onto when all the supports have been pulled away?

> Fear not, for I have redeemed you;
> I have called you by name, you are mine.
> When you pass through the waters
> I will be with you;
> and through the rivers, they shall not overwhelm
> you.... (Is 43:1-2)

A new heart I will give you,
and a new spirit I will put within you;
and I will take out of your flesh the heart of stone
and give you a heart of flesh. (Ez 36:26)

God is the ground of hope. It is God finally who enables us to start over.

As Hebrew scripture scholar Walter Brueggemann reminds us, prophetic speech was meant to lead the community of faith to two difficult but crucial moves, *relinquishment* and *receiving*. The community had to let go of the old world of king and temple to receive from God a new world it could not conceive. And it had to give up an idolatrous order of public life to embrace a new mode of communal existence. As Brueggemann makes clear, the full impact of discouragement is often a call to conversion.[8]

Heartened by beauty

There is another way to lighten our discouragement over the evils in the world. That is to take in the beauty and joy of the universe as fully as possible. We have personally found this an essential antidote to heaviness of heart. After listening all day as counselors to people pouring out their anguish, and hearing again how human beings harm one another—through rape, abuse, cruelty, and neglect—we need to experience again the goodness of the world. We find it at times in moments with nature. Rather than simply walking past a blossoming plum tree or a freshly blooming rose, we stop to really see the fresh promise of this flowering. Sometimes in the midst of hard times it is the stillness of water at sunset, the sight of a squadron of pelicans at play, or the song of a robin that restores and heals us.

We notice as well the small acts of kindness that human beings offer to one another on the bus or in the grocery store—a stranger giving a hand to a mother trying to juggle both groceries and a small baby, young people volunteering to do yard work for a sick neighbor, friends rallying around a family who have lost their home in a fire. Or we may meet the beauty and resilience of the human spirit in a poem, a symphony, a painting, a novel. These too are part of creation, portrayals of our capacity both to love and to fail in loving.

It is striking how the Psalms move, in the midst of painful protest against personal and societal evil, to a focus on the wonders of creation. They accurately portray the darkness: "Every cave in the land is a place where violence has made its home (74:20)"; "I see nothing but violence and strife in the city (55:9)." Then suddenly they call us to wonder and praise at the sheer goodness of the world. In the Psalms, God calls the stars by name, sends rain to put fresh grass on the hillsides, and spreads snow on the earth like a blanket.

Our weary spirits need to take all the nourishment they can from the beauty of the world. Even small moments of it can eventually flower into hope for us and our planet.

Prayer

Teach us, O God, to trust in your future for the earth.
Throughout time you have taught your people to
hope and be strong, to laugh and to dance.

We remember the people of the Exodus, how they wan-
dered in the desert losing direction and heart. You
led them to an oasis. You were the water they
drank, the rock on whom they could rely.

We remember the guests at the wedding in Cana, where
the wine ran low and then ran out. They had no
wine. Then, suddenly, gallons of it!

We remember Mary of Nazareth, the peasant girl who
asked, "How can this be?" Her faith was not in
things seen. She said yes to you, and sang of the
new creation.

We remember Jacob, who wrestled with you until dawn,
emerged wounded yet encouraged, and heard you
promise to be with him wherever he went.

You, O God, are our hope in time of despair. Keep us safe
from despondency's grip. May we hold fast to
your promises.

–Kathleen Fischer and Thomas Hart

Chapter Six

Encouraging One Another

*S*trengthen all weary hands,
steady all trembling knees,
and say to all faint hearts,
"Courage! Do not be afraid."
—Isaiah 35:3–4

A few years ago Tom decided to write my mother a special letter for her birthday. It had been a difficult year for her. My dad had suffered a second stroke and, after she had tried unsuccessfully to care for him, had to be moved to a nursing home. Six months later he died. In the letter, Tom told my mother the things he appreciated about her: her resilience of spirit, her generosity and sense of gratitude, the hard work she had done over the years, like canning and cleaning into the night after the last kids were in bed. My mother treasured the letter, sharing it with several of my brothers and sisters. And then she set out to do the same for others. She began writing us cards with the positive things she wanted to tell us: "Why should you have to wait till you're dead to have people say these things?" she said.

As we make our way through life, trying to do our best but aware how often we fail, words of encouragement buoy us up and renew our energy. At times the light in our hearts goes out, and we owe a deep debt to those who fan it into flame again. Encouragement can take many forms, but it often includes extending help, showing appreciation, believing in others. It is God's own love we incarnate in giving others heart.

Giving and receiving help

Once while visiting China, where every imaginable method of transporting goods is employed, we watched the effect of lifting another's burden. An old woman staggered slowly along the street, a large basket of vegetables attached to her back. Her head and body were bent forward under the strain. Then two uniformed schoolgirls walking behind her stepped up to grasp the bottom of the basket on each side, sharing its weight as they matched the rhythm of her steps. The woman looked around, startled, then slowly smiled at them as she saw the reason for the lightening of her load.

We live in a society where the Lone Ranger model of strength still prevails. Being an adult is equated with being as independent as possible. Pull yourself up by your own bootstraps, we are told. Asking for help, depending on another, admitting that you need someone—these are signs of weakness to avoid. No wonder we so often feel alone, overwhelmed, hopeless. Discouragement thrives in isolation. It is the sense that we are on our own, even when our resources are inadequate. The cry of our hearts, "I can't do it anymore," is often this sense of solitariness.

Hope, on the other hand, flourishes in community. It is the sense that help is near, like finding a lighthouse with a steady beacon when we are at sea. Hope thrives among people who sense their mutual openness to one another, those who see life as a web of help given and received.

Community is especially crucial when we face suffering and loss. In *The Gifts of the Body*, her collection of stories about assisting people dying from *AIDS*, home-care worker Rebecca Brown tells us how even the smallest details of life can become a process of giving and receiving, gifts exchanged around the most elemental of human needs. Brown takes us on her rounds as she cooks a meal, cleans house, does laundry, helps a person bathe. In and through these gestures, she shows us how we sustain hope in one another, even in the face of death. Rick, one of the men she bathes and cooks for, loves cinnamon rolls from the Hostess eatery a few blocks from where he lives. On one of her visits Rick wants to surprise her, so he gathers all his strength to walk to the Hostess and bring back two soft, sticky cinnamon rolls. He sets them out with two dessert plates in his kitchen. However, the effort exhausts him completely; he cannot share the meal. Brown writes:

"He'd laid the table hopefully. I took the food he meant for me, I ate."[9]

Showing appreciation

We lose heart when our efforts are not acknowledged. A mother carefully prepares a meal and watches her family gulp it down without a word before they head off to the TV or computer. An employee gives his best to a company project, and his boss grabs the praise. An aide in a nursing home is gentle and effective with a resident, but never hears even a simple thank you. How often has your own discouragement come from not knowing whether anyone even noticed?

Appreciation lets us know that we really matter. It need not wait on special actions. After all, the greatest gift is simply another person's presence. It only takes a moment to let someone know they mean a lot to us: "I'm so glad I have you for a daughter." "What a joy it is to know you." "You are special to me and I love you." Whatever else is happening in our lives, these words, when spoken from the heart, give us energy to go on, to try again, to wrestle with obstacles.

We find many places where Saint Paul describes the practice of encouraging one another as a way of strengthening the community that Jesus came to establish. As a basis for appreciating one another, Paul offers us the analogy of a body where every part, no matter how small or seemingly insignificant, has a special function:

> If all the parts were the same, how could it be a body? As it is, the parts are many but the body is

one. The eye cannot say to the hand, "I do not need you," nor can the head say to the feet, "I do not need you." What is more, it is precisely the parts of the body that seem the weakest which are the indispensable ones....(l Cor 12:19–23)

In leading up to this analogy, Paul names the variety of gifts with which the Spirit blesses the community: the speaking of wisdom, the utterance of knowledge, faith, gifts of healing, prophecy, discernment of spirits (1 Cor 12:7–11). In his letters he continually gives thanks to members of the community for sharing their gifts, and asks us all to extend this kind of thanks to one another.

There are countless ways in which we inadvertently limit the life in one other and in ourselves. The expression of appreciation reverses that negative energy, empowering everyone so that all the gifts are released into the community.

Believing in another

Sometimes we lift the discouragement from the hearts of others by reawakening the sense that they can meet the challenges of life. Anne Lamott's best-selling work on writing, *Bird by Bird,* draws its title from a lovely story of such encouragement. Thirty years ago, she says, her brother, who was ten years old at the time, was trying to get a report on birds written that he'd had three months to write. It was due the next day. He was at the kitchen table surrounded by binder paper, pencils, and unopened books on birds, close to tears, paralyzed by the hugeness of

WISDOM

KNOWLEDGE

FAITH

HEALING

PROPHECY

DISCERNMENT

the task. Then Anne's father sat down beside him, put his arm around his shoulder, and said, "Bird by bird, buddy. Just take it bird by bird."[10]

There is a folk saying that tells us: A friend is someone who knows the song in your heart, and sings it back to you when you have forgotten how it goes. Each of us loses faith in ourselves at times. How important it is then to have someone mirror back to us the qualities we have forgotten. For some of us this person might have been a teacher who glimpsed the future we could not see, as we found ourselves too short or too tall, too quick or too slow to fit in with the rest of our classmates. It might have been a friend who said, "You can do it!" when the obstacles to a new job or relationship seemed daunting. Perhaps it was a grandparent or favorite aunt or uncle who never gave up on us, no matter how much trouble we seemed to cause.

The community of faith also plays this role. The spiritual journey needs the context of a community to uphold us when our personal energies flag. We were struck by how true this is while talking with a man in his eighties. Recently he had to move from his home into a retirement apartment. When asked how he is doing, he invariably replies: "Not so good. I'm not worth much these days." But sometimes when we see him he is positive and energetic, laughs easily, and looks like a different person. These are the days he works as a volunteer at a shelter for the homeless. The staff respect and like him. That, and the service itself, provide a tonic no medicine can supply.

The face of God

Perhaps the deepest source of encouragement is to know that God looks on us, and all our flawed efforts, with love. We listened to a woman plagued by the conviction that God must be very disappointed in her and what she has done with her life. As we talked, it became clear that her God was almost exclusively the harsh master in Luke's parable of the talents (19:ll–27). This God was continually judging her actions and finding that she did not measure up to expectations. She had almost no sense of a divine face of compassion and delight.

How do we envision the face of God turned toward us? Can we open ourselves to the God of gracious love and compassion who struggles with us against the pain of the world? As Brian Wren, the hymn-maker, leads us in singing,

> Dear Sister God,
>   you held me at my birth.
> You sang my name, were glad to see my face.
>   You are my sky, my shining sun,
> and in your love there's always room
>   to be, and grow, yet find a home,
> a settled place.[11]

This song captures the bible's witness to a God who rejoices in our creation, seeing that all is very good (Gn 1:31), a God who calls us by name and in whose eyes we are precious (Hos 11:1–5), a God who offers us unlimited forgiveness.

If you never overlooked our sins, Yahweh,
    could anyone survive?
But you do forgive us;
    and for that we revere you. (Ps 130:3–4)

When we lose heart, it is to such a God that we need to return. This is the One who knows us intimately, accepts us completely, and loves us tenderly, weeping with us in our pain, upholding us in our struggles, forgiving us our failings. This is the friend who is the ultimate source of our encouragement.

Prayer

May the Breath of the Spirit clear a nurturing space within
you, and fill it with joy in your gifts;

May the power of Jesus' resurrection break the bonds that
imprison you, and free you from your frustrations
and fears;

May the graciousness of God embrace and comfort you,
and stir in you fresh energy for the tasks at hand.
—Kathleen Fischer and Thomas Hart

Notes

1. Etty Hillesum, *An Interrupted Life* (New York: Simon & Schuster, 1985), 241–42.

2. G. K. Chesterton, *Orthodoxy* (New York: Doubleday, l959), 50.

3. Marchiene Vroon Rienstra, *Swallow's Nest: A Feminine Reading of the Psalms* (Michigan: William B. Eerdmans, 1992), 85.

4. Georges Bernanos, *Diary of a Country Priest* (New York: Doubleday, 1954), 233.

5. Julie McHale, "Butterflies," unpublished poem.

6. "God's Grandeur," in W. H. Gardner, ed., *Poems and Prose of Gerard Manley Hopkins* (Baltimore: Penguin, 1953), 27.

7. Linda Hogan, *Dwellings: A Spiritual History of the Living World* (New York: Simon & Schuster, 1996), 33.

8. Walter Brueggemann, *Hopeful Imagination: Prophetic Voices in Exile* (Philadelphia: Fortress, 1986), 3–7.

9. Rebecca Brown, *The Gifts of the Body* (New York: HarperCollins, 1994), 10.

10. Anne Lamott, *Bird by Bird* (New York: Pantheon, 1994), 19.

11. Brian Wren, *God-Talk in Worship: A Male Response to Feminist Theology* (New York: Crossroad, 1989), 164.